CHOP WOOD, CARRY WATER

The Yoga of Work

ANDREW TAGGART

To my wife Alexandra,
who taught me to love what is.

Before Enlightenment, chop wood, carry water. After Enlightenment, chop wood, carry water.
Modern Zen Saying

The sense of doership is the bondage and not the actions themselves.
Ramana Maharshi, *Be As You Are*

Through work you go beyond work.
Swami Satprakashananda, *Mind According to Vedanta*

CONTENTS

INTRODUCTION

I have given them your word, and the world has hated them because they are not of the world, just as I am not of the world. I do not ask that you take them out of the world, but that you keep them from the evil one. They are not of the world, just as I am not of the world.

–Jesus, John 17:14-16

'I AM NOT OF THE WORLD'

Jesus's words to his disciples, crackling with energy and fiercely truthful, have resounded in many a person's ears over the millennia, not the least my own. One of the existential themes that's stuck, like a barnacle, to me (a "natural koan" as my Zen teacher would, decades later, have put it) has been a persistent feeling of existential homelessness. A few lyrics from Radiohead's "Creep" have touched me deeply: "I'm a weirdo. / What the hell am I doin' here? / I don't belong here."

Who hasn't felt as if he doesn't belong here, and how many have sought transcendence in one form or another? When Jesus urges his disciples to refuse to be "of the world," we might read him as telling us moderns that the modern world's dominant values such as pleasure, power, wealth, and status needn't, indeed *shouldn't*, be our own. From a deeply spiritual point of view, we can take him as encouraging us to turn inward in order to realize that "the kingdom of heaven is within." "Yes!," our hearts might cry out. "Yes! Yes!"

Taking this call for renunciation seriously, we may then go into "the heart of the desert" and live, for a time, in actual solitude or, at least, in a space of quietude. Such a recommendation, in fact, is frequently made in many scriptures or sacred texts, which enjoin seekers to withdraw from sense pleasures and, at times too, from social engagements so that the spiritual quest within can not only be undertaken but can also fructify.

All this sounds amazing until one has to do

the dishes, or fill out tax forms, or wait in line for hours. Thus, at our peril do contemplatives overlook two very simple facts, which can readily become places of "spiritual nesting." The first is that action in general and work in particular are—just like thoughts, feelings, sensations, and perceptions—appearing over and over again. Accordingly, work, of some kind or another, cannot be avoided irrespective of one's contemplative leanings. Work will always find you out as though it were hunting you down. Therefore, renunciation of the world's values cannot mean the refusal to "chop wood, carry water." Unpacking what this line means will be the chief purpose of this book.

The second fact is that one is to love all beings, yet how is this possible so long as one is living in solitude? Work is that ongoing endeavor that invites me, in my dealings with others, not to treat them as other but to love them verily "as myself." How it's possible to overcome one's nasty little dislikes of other beings is the subject of Chapters 7-9.

So far from the world being a hindrance, it is—if, that is, the yoga of work is properly understood—to be a helpmate. Isn't it true that we begin to recognize just where we're caught, stuck, or holding onto ego in virtue of our re-

lationships both with tasks and with other beings—be they cockroaches, mosquitos, dogs, or
humans?

Jesus never told his disciples to take flight.

'I AM IN THE WORLD'

It's fitting that, by the eighteenth and
nineteenth centuries, Jesus's words came to be
formulated as an epigram that, revealing a ten-
sion, also advanced a daring ethical demand:
one is *not* to be *of* the world, and yet one is to
be *in* it. Everything we care about hangs deli-
cately on this "and yet."

One of the most powerful ideas, starting,
perhaps, with the Renaissance and reaching a
watershed moment during the Enlightenment,
is the modern commitment to human auton-
omy. Today, one is to be an agent who acts for
the sake of the ends he articulates, chief
among which is the transformation of the
world. For Karl Marx, Georg Wilhelm
Friedrich Hegel's serious flaw was that he was
bound to an outdated view of philosophy as
contemplation. In words that are now famous,
Marx accused both Hegel and Ludvig Feuerbach of capitulation to the status quo: "The
philosophers," he intoned in his eleventh
thesis on Feuerbach, "have only interpreted

the world, in various ways; the point is to change it."

See that? "[T]he point is to change it." It's impossible not to envision, when hearing this statement, all of these and more: the French Revolution, the American Revolution, colonial and postcolonial struggles, as well as paradigm-changing technological innovations like the steam engine, the internet, and now AI. In fact, it can feel as if modernity is itself "liquid" (to borrow a metaphor from Zygmunt Bauman) and, yes, as if–Marx again–"all that is solid melts into air."

Our time, it can hardly be understated, is a time of action. Our heroes are self-authoring, our villains culpable. Our cities, as much as our artworks, consist of the ideas that are to be made manifest in countless, and countlessly malleable, forms. The modern human–self-propelled and self-fashioning in the process–is a maker, a doer, a wonder. One is, finally, to be a self-transforming dynamo, a god unto himself.

Karma yoga, as I'll argue in this book, begs to differ–but in a very compassionate and dexterous way. On the one hand, it curbs the enthusiasm of *would-be or wannabe* world deniers or world renouncers like me, those who have made the mistake of thinking that turning away from the world completely entails being transcendently free. It does not. It is just here that selfless service makes its presence felt. On the other hand, since the energy of our time is movement, action, whirling, work, karma yoga tries to "spiritualize" this tendency by turning it into ongoing opportunities to *overcome one's selfish proclivities*. In other words, action, from this vantage point, is the spur not for endless outwardness but for a much-needed inward turn.

Thus, karma yoga, a form of inner purification, offers an antidote for the proclivities of *both* contemplatives *and* world changers. To the first, it says: "Your work is not done. You must see all the suffering that's bound up with your allergies to action and other beings, and you must let all this suffering dissolve *through the very mundane activities that you have hitherto sworn off.* You are, for instance, to stop sneering at your assignment, which is to chop wood, and instead you are to let it be chopped with equanimity." To the second, it says, "You cannot continue to act without taking up the examination of the quality of action, your thirst for personal gain, and your unwillingness to open yourself to the true and only author, who is divine. Action is to be your salvation because by means of action your pride will be smashed. Through humility, your heart shall be opened."

In short, the yoga of work corrects contemplatives by empowering them, through a deeper examination of their attachments and aversions, to *turn outward*, at the same time that it teaches doers, by virtue of their confrontation with their own dissatisfaction, to *turn inward*. Both, in fact, come to discover that the real work *is*, in the final analysis, the inner work. The real work is to work with work in order to go beyond work. What this message entails is to be spelled out over the course of this short, modern rendition of karma yoga: the yoga of work.

THIS IS A LOVE STORY

Chop Wood, Carry Water is ultimately a love story. As with any good love story, the beginning is far from the ending.

In *Shawshank Redemption* (1994), a film, set in 1948, that depicts the lives of inmates with long prison sentences, Andy Dufresne, wrongly convicted of murdering his wife and her lover, devotes years of his life to finding a way to escape from Shawshank. Near the end, he breaks through his cell wall and subsequently crawls through a sewage pipe that's 500 yards long.

The parallel between Andy's long crawl to freedom and the yoga of work is striking. Through work, we can come face to face with daily trials and tribulations. Through work, we can free ourselves from the very afflictions that are mind-created. And we don't just face these trials; we crawl through them. Indeed, through work, we *can* come—beyond attachments, beyond aversions, beyond desires, and, above all, beyond pride—to a wise love. This is not the innocent love of youth but the mature, gracious love that has ultimately transcended mundane hardships.

How To Read This Book

At the beginning of almost every chapter, practical pointers are included with a view to guiding you as you embrace the challenges, and blessings, of work. Each is an invitation to interpret a certain situation in the light of this cue. For instance, the pointer—"Observe: 'To be honest, I dislike this.'"—is reminding you to carefully inspect the aversion or allergy *right as it appears*. Other pointers are urging you to attend to different salient features that surround mundane tasks. All of them, when taken to-gether, are offering up nothing less than *a transformation of your basic attitude toward* work. If they're taken as prompts for practice, then you can gradually come to an experiential un-derstanding of what it's like for wood to chop itself, for water to carry itself, and for emails to write themselves. Through this slow, beautiful inner purification, you can know ease and then too love. You can, in short, find life *good*.

HEAPS AND
MISADVENTURES

A QUIET BEAUTY

The Indian sage Ramana Maharshi states, "Let action take place of its own accord." And according to a modern Zen saying, "Before Enlightenment, chop wood, carry water. After Enlightenment, chop wood, carry water."

Much of what I wish to convey in this book can be found, in condensed form, in these two astonishing statements. Both are suggesting that the affairs of ordinary life are to be carried out with a certain attitude—indeed, with a certain *experiential understanding* that need not speak its name. Neither, in fact, even remotely implies that the events that make up our ordinary lives—and certainly not the various kinds of work that comprise much of our days—are going to change, or at least not very much.

Ramana Maharshi still wakes up early to chop vegetables, and the Zen master is still seen carrying a heavy bucket of water from the rushing stream. The proclamation that the happenings in our lives won't likely change may sound gloomy, but it's anything but that. On the contrary, what is felt by the one who truly grasps the essence of the yoga of work is a quiet beauty, an energy that's unfolding through seamless activity. For such a one, there is not just ease but also love.

We cannot, however, begin at the end—with simple, resistance-free brushstrokes gracing the white page; with axes splitting hickory and buckets carrying spring water; with calm, unperturbed smiles shining through days of meetings—but with where we are. We have, as it turns out, to start right here in the muck.

Heaps of Burdens

I'd like to begin by sketching two cases that are so commonplace that they can be, and therefore often are, easily overlooked. The first one I call "heaps of burdens"; the second "a cascade of misadventures."

Imagine: *all* you wanted to do was to *just* go and finish this task when, en route, you noticed that A, then also B, and then too C, not to mention D needs to be taken care of. For example, you were *just* going to take out the compost or the trash when you noticed a plant in need of watering, litter strewn about, a rain barrel leaking, and little packages of wrapped-up dog poop lying here and there. Remember: you'd *told yourself* that there was one very pointed task to be completed when out of the blue, you were forced to confront the heaps of tasks—all different, sometimes quite varied—that had, behind your back, begun to pile up. How could this have happened?

It gets worse: more sensitive scanning of the situation reveals that there are *more tasks*—dead branches to be cut down, a new oak to be watered separately—calling for your attention, others that you'll have to relegate to "later" or "tomorrow" or to some other list entirely.

It's worth pausing here to take stock of what this developing scenario *feels like*. Go back: you started off with *a sense of ease, clarity, and direction*; you believed that what lay ahead was going to be *easy*; and you discovered en route a feeling of being weighed down by the difference between your initial intention ("Just take out the trash and come right back.") and the accounting that transpired along the way (the plants, the litter, the rain barrel, the dog poop, the hose, the weeds...). You didn't just feel burdened by the acknowledgement of one errant thing; you felt burdened (does it linger still as you recall it?) because your overly dramatic, almost histrionic re-assessment is that there's *always more* to get done and *never* enough time or capacity to do it. Who is going to do all this? And when? And how?

A gentle breeze—or a stiff wind—of not just *overwhelm* but also, and more potently, *futility* may be setting in. How can you not hear a faint demonic thought whispering that your efforts may be futile or that life's tasks could be—or at least seem to be—too much for you to bear? As you were *just about* to chop wood, lo and behold: a broken water pail, undressed kids, an unfinished report, and the pressing need (think of the recent Amazon layoffs) to get up to speed on AI.

Naturally, for one who takes seriously the heaps of burdens cases, life may very well come to feel—as many conversation partners with whom I philosophize have reported—like a grind or a slog, a blur or a whirl. I'll come to this attitude below when I speak about "the ordeal."

A CASCADE OF MISADVENTURES

But now I must come to the second case. While the first one spotlights the quixotic problem of quantity whereby "one task horrifically begets ten," the second brings the problem of errancy sharply into focus. How so? Let's suppose that you *just* (that word again) want to download a certain app in order, you note, to *just* do this very simple thing with it. But it turns out that you don't have enough memory available on your phone, so you go about deleting old apps. At which point, you go back and download the original app, and then realize that something or other isn't compatible with your camera. Or maybe it *is* compatible, but the picture quality isn't as great as you'd hoped. And, well, the pictures you *did* take with it a moment ago you can't seem to figure out how to upload, so you need to use Generative AI or ChatGPT to locate the hidden buttons, or you have to flip through YouTube videos—each short, each promising to be helpful—to learn how to do this... I could keep going on in this vein, but I trust you get the point.

Whereas in the heaps of burdens case the initial task, being easy, is nonetheless hounded by *other* tasks that surround it, the misadventures case draws out your miscalculation about the pointiness of the task in question. In both cases, your expectations are confounded. In both, your composure is challenged and, depending on your particular threshold, quite possibly shattered.

NOT SO SIMPLE, NOT SO EASY…

My hunch is that you've told yourself over and over again that "this is going to be simple and straightforward" *and* that you've failed to see that, as a matter of fact, the heaps of burdens *and* the misadventures cases both run wild. In other words, *far from being anomalous, merely accidental, or only occasional, they are nearly ubiquitous.* Look around you. A careful inspection of the work you do on a daily basis will, I suggest, bear this claim out.

What do these cases have to say about our basic attitudes toward work?

❧ 2 ❧

LIFE FEELS HARD

POINTER 1: OBSERVE: "LIFE FEELS HARD."

LIFE AS AN ORDEAL

Perhaps what God says to Adam and Eve, after the Fall, is not so far from the truth. Eve's punishment for having eaten the forbidden fruit is to know that "with painful labor you will give birth to children" (Genesis 3:16) while Adam, no longer a happy gatherer, is to become a farmer: "through painful toil you will eat food from it / all the days of your life" (Genesis 3:17). Who hasn't felt that work—whether it involves caring for children or managing a small team—is "painful toil"?

No one can immediately bear the strain of work without adopting some attitude toward it. Before, in the final chapter, I lay out my view of a realistic Taoist understanding, I'll range over the two dominant and ultimately unwise stances we can take.

The first is to succumb to *gloomy pessimism* and thus to believe that *life itself is an ordeal.* Accepting that we're all thrown into a fallen world, you believe you're being courageous by facing the darkness, and yet you're often looking for consolation and reassurance from others. Your complaints about the world being broken due to the unremitting cycle of cease-less toil are to be ameliorated by anyone who sees your pain. Yet this reassurance is short-lived, the gloom returns, and the one who sought to console you feels her own mood be-coming darker as a result.

To ensure that I'm not speaking at a level that's too abstract, my suggestion, just now, will be that we visualize the following scenario. It's been a long yet fruitful day, and you imagine yourself sitting down in your favorite chair where you'll be reading an enriching book. But just before you sit down, you glance at the sink in which are stacked, one atop the other, more than a few dirty dishes. Try to stay with this mental image. The very next thought, however subtle it may be, will be something like this: "Life *feels* hard." Really *feel* that emotion: "Life *feels* hard." In this emotion is contained a precious truth about an attitude you've adopted, probably at various moments during the course of your life, but have almost always overlooked. The essence of this attitude is that life is an ordeal. Can you really welcome this arising, "Life *feels* hard," without any judgment and without turning away from it?

Be present with what's present while placing the emphasis—the accent mark, a glowing attention—on *your being the one* who is present with this feeling. In other words, be the observer knowingly, steadily, wakefully.

❧ 3 ❧
SOMEWHERE, SOMEDAY, I WILL BE HAPPY

POINTER 2: OBSERVE: "IN SOME OTHER WORLD, I WILL BE HAPPY."

DREAMSCAPES AND FANTASIES

In contrast with gloomy pessimism, a second stance, in which one turns steadily away from the burdensomeness of mundane tasks, involves projecting dreamscapes and fantasies. The English philosopher and novelist Iris Murdoch cautions us against indulging in the near-constant fantasies that we too readily get lost in.

This raises a question: "If it's true—and it is—that we're prone to daydreams, fantasies, and reveries, why do we find them all so enticing?" Because, in a word, they offer passing pleasure, a moment of relief. Sometimes we envision a time without or beyond work as toil while at other times we call up dream jobs, dream projects, grand callings, beautiful collaborations, and epic workscapes. Either way, we've momentarily slipped away from the idea that life is an ordeal.

The sun *will* come out and so beautifully tomorrow, won't it? But will it *stay up*? Will it shine *continuously*? Will we, through fantasy, truly be happy?

Just as we zeroed in on the "felt sense" of life being an ordeal by allowing an ancient voice to say, "Life *feels* so very hard," so too we can fine-tune our experiential grasp of dreamscapes by inviting a second voice to speak. This one says, "In some other world, I will feel happy and shall finally be whole."

To hear this voice as clearly as possible, first imagine a mundane task from which you often turn away (perhaps the word that springs to mind is "avoidance" or "procrastination"). Then really take note of the *next* thought, feeling, or action: you simply find yourself, don't you?, looking at a polished, highly curated "beautiful life" on Instagram, or else remembering a charming time when you were young, or thinking fondly of a sailboat you'll someday fix up and sail.

My emphasis here is not on the usual terms like "distraction" or "procrastination" but is rather on the *dreamlike, pleasing quality* of this reverie, the felt sense of happiness, wholeness, or rest. Can you let go of this particular image and be open to the possibility that your current experience, here and now and without any thoughts, is happy, complete, or at peace? See for yourself.

A SEVERE TRIAL

Know that I have no interest in denigrating these two attitudes, only, to begin with, in entreating us to see them and to take note of both. Don't we all tend to feel the hardness of life and then, and this quite quickly, the siren song of a better world so wondrously beckoning us?

Yet this is not all. Remember that we're looking very closely at the phenomenology of work—at what it's actually like to catch a glimpse of a mundane task. So far, our discoveries have been nothing short of striking: the first attitude, biblical in its resonance, casts life as an ordeal—a "severe trial," a "test of courage, strength, or endurance," suggests the etymology—while the second, turning starkly away from this darkness, projects fictional, pleasant light over yonder.

If we wish to know what it means to chop wood and carry water with ease, grace, and love, then we had better press on with our inquiry.

✻ 4 ✻

I'LL NEVER BE OR HAVE
ENOUGH

**POINTER 3: PROBE: "I'M AFRAID I'LL
NEVER HAVE OR BE ENOUGH."**

PRIMAL FEAR

Let's, in fact, go one step further. As we scrape off life both as an ordeal and as a delusional fantasy, what is hereby exposed? Quite often deep, possibly revolting fear–fear either of not having enough or (in the case of one for whom work is the means by which he achieves success or recognition) of not being or becoming enough.

When you "stare through" this mundane task, there may be, "on the other side," a rustling, a shuttering, a quaking of the spirit.

"I'll never, ever have enough," says this primitive voice. "I won't be struck down by a catastrophe. No, I'll slowly wither away and die, and all those I love, and who are dependent upon me, will follow in train." Or else it says, "I'll never prove my worth, value, or significance in the eyes of my titan-peers. I'll never make my mark or leave my dent in the universe. I'll never really make it, and thus what I see staring at me is complete, irreversible, disgraceful failure: a stigmata."

How astonishing it is that something as commonplace, as mundane as a simple task can be, if we look closely and if we remain dispassionate during our looking, a site of such spiritual depth, of such inner torment!

It's enough to simply open to this experience of fear. In the same way that you, the subject, perceive a tree, an object, you can observe any emotion—quietly, openly, lovingly. While fear may be more intense than the sight of a maple tree, both are objects that *you observe*. Both, therefore, are *separate* from your being. Fear, just like any other emotion or thought, is inviting you to knowingly stand *as the observer* who, like a vast background, is attending to this experience. Thus, the invitation is to open—no more, no less—to the experience of being afraid of never having, or being, enough. Just see what this is like.

After we've taken careful note of the ordeal, the fantasy of happiness, and the primal fear, we're now in a position to reflect upon our unwillingness, just so long as we subscribe to either the burden character of existence or the dream of happiness "out there," to carefully *stay with* the mundane nature of modern work. When we persevere with the mundane task, we'll see that there's quiet beauty here. The alternative view that I will espouse, one that will introduce us to karma yoga (or what I'm terming "the yoga of work"), will take honest self-reckoning as its starting point.

BEING HONEST WITH YOURSELF

POINTER 4: OBSERVE: "TO BE HONEST, I DISLIKE THIS."

PRETENSE AND HONESTY

Let's circle back to the biblical *mythos* in order to get our bearings. Notice that God's punishment mandates that Adam and Eve both be engaged in seemingly endless work—thirsty fields yearning for water, screaming children hungry again—in order for them to persist in their existence. Haven't we too felt that work is unavoidable yet also—in an eerily uncanny way that resembles Chinese water torture—almost unbearable?

Is there any liberation that comes on the

heels of this acknowledgement? Yes, there is, but the only means by which one can come to deep, living wisdom is to accept, at the outset, that we *really don't like* something—which is to admit that we *really have* suffered.

Most people, time and time again, are refusing this admission. Instead, they *pretend* that they love work, or that they love their work, and then they go one step further and *tell others* that they love work or that they especially love their work. The problem is that they're not looking closely enough at their actual experiences: the resistances, the indecisions, the constipations (so to speak), the avoidances, the reticences, the heel-draggings, the vacillations, the endlessly made-up dilemmas, the melodramas, the self-pitying, the myriad forms of stuckness, the dead-ends, the hideouts, the petty angers, the nitpickings, and on and on. How is it possible to love anyone or anything wholeheartedly when you've not taken stock of how, on a moment-by-moment basis, you *actually feel?*

To say to yourself, "To be honest, I dislike this," is the very first step in the modern version of karma yoga that I'm envisioning. I'm not urging you to shout about this moment of honest insight from the top of some building, or to turn toward a colleague and share this dirty little secret. I'm inviting you to stop telling yourself what Henrik Ibsen called "life-lies," to give up all the bullshit.

This moment of honesty may not seem like much, but it is, in truth, a most remarkable thing. The very thing you've not articulated is now placed right in front of you. Clarity is disburdening, slowly freeing. To see the obvious yet overlooked is perhaps one of the greatest moments of wisdom.

With fresh eyes, then, you can look at work in a totally different way: not, in the first place, as that arena in which you prove yourself and thus achieve success but instead as a spiritual stage upon which your resistances and your desires, being brought before you, are slowly *worked out*. In brief, the yoga of work is the working out of your stuff. Let's see how.

❧ 6 ❧

KARMA YOGA, OLD
SCHOOL AND NEW

**POINTER 5: VERIFY: "WORK IS NEARLY
EVERYWHERE."**

**POINTER 6: CONFIRM: "THE BASIC UNIT
OF MODERN WORK IS THE MUNDANE
TASK."**

FOR THE BIGHEARTED ONLY?

The standard view of karma yoga is succinctly expounded by Swami Prabhavananda and Christopher Isherwood in *How to Know God: The Yoga Aphorisms of Patanjali*. They write:

Karma yoga is the path of selfless, God-dedicated action. By dedicating the fruits of one's work to God, and by working always with the right means toward right ends..., one may gradually achieve wisdom and non-attachment.

As we would expect, they note that this type of path is attractive to highly extroverted people with big hearts. Thus: "Karma yoga," they aver, "is the path best suited to vigorous temperaments which feel the call to duty and service in the world of human affairs." For this reason, when we think of karma yoga in this vein, we picture tireless religious figures and social reformers like Mother Theresa, Gandhi, Florence Nightingale, and St. Francis of Assisi, and, as a result of these imaginative flights, we may conclude that we have no business trying to *be* karma yogis since humanitarian heroism or ecological activism is not our forte.

To be sure, we wouldn't be wrong to draw such a conclusion, *provided that we accepted unquestionably the standard view*, but we could be making a crucial mistake by overlooking a striking opportunity, one, in fact, that's staring us right in the face.

This slightly unorthodox view of karma yoga—the yoga of work—will seek to take into account, as its point of departure, two basic facts about the modern world. First, one can't avoid doing work, of some sort or another, on any given day. By "work," I mean whatever efforts are undertaken in order to maintain these *bodies*. To be sure, certain kinds of work become increasingly sophisticated, and livelihoods become more rarified as modern society—industrialized, then digitized, now swiftly becoming AI'd—becomes more complex, but never do these depart from their stake in the ground, which is the transient nature of these hungry, thirsty, needy bodies.

On this account, dreaming up a new business with the help of ChatGPT counts as work *just as much* as picking up dog or baby toys drenched in saliva. Indeed, work of various kinds—bringing your car in for routine service, checking up on lab results, washing dishes, brushing your teeth, attending Zoom meetings, sending out a report, taking a call, reshaping a design prompt, pulling weeds during a silent Zen retreat—*beckons* in sundry ways throughout the course of the day. And, much to your surprise, the closer and more carefully you look, the more you start to take note of this overlooked fact that you are, upon waking up, working *almost constantly!*

Second—and here, I think, is the beginning of a real twist—the modern world in particular offers us what I'll call "mundane tasks" in spades. The late David Graeber, in his book *Bullshit Jobs*, may have marveled at capitalism's ability, at least up until 2018, to create the sorts of meaningless, needless, thankless jobs that do nothing of any relevance, but he failed to spot something that's far more prevalent and that couldn't be any more obvious: the *ubiquitous* nature of mundane tasks.

These two facts—a) work is nearly everywhere, and b) the basic unit of modern work is decidedly not the epic project or the sweeping vision of heaven on earth but the utterly mundane task—together invite us to rethink *what karma yoga is in modernity*: that is to say, which unique gauntlet it's throwing down for us.

Which brings us forthwith to the way in which mundane tasks persistently surface our mental problems. In the next three chapters, we'll be looking closely at the real work of work, which is none other than cleaning up the mind.

❧ 7 ❧

CLEANING UP THE
MIND, PART 1: TENSIONS
AND TENDENCIES

POINTER 7: SEE YOUR TENSIONS AND TENDENCIES.

POINTER 8: CONTEMPLATE: "THE REAL WORK OF WORK IS THE CLEARING OF THE MIND."

TENSIONS AND TENDENCIES

In a voluminous book on various types of yoga entitled *Yoga and Kriya: A Systematic Course in the Ancient Tantric Techniques*, Swami Satyananda Saraswati and fellow contributors observe:

> Karma yoga is a means to clean out the mind of phobias, problems, fears and all other disturbing factors. During karma yoga, a person has to face all types of experiences, whether good or bad.

They continue, "[I]t is very difficult to find your mental problems when there is no interaction with other people." Their pregnant suggestion—that is, that the great boon of the field of work is that, perhaps more readily than in the context of seated meditation practice, it often forcefully reveals our mental blocks—is one that I'd like to flesh out in what follows.

It's thanks to work of all kinds that, from a spiritual point of view, you're given an in-your-face opportunity to "really see your own shit." Work makes this "seeing your own shit" *very obvious* since all the resistances plus all the fantasies are revealed in the blooming of the imagination and in the grip of strong emotions.

In order for us to see our own stuff very keenly *and* to start putting it down very slowly, let's focus our attention, in this chapter, on two categories: tensions and tendencies. Following immediately after any strong dislike, tensions are felt *inside the body* while tendencies are evident in our *thoughts and feelings*. Tensions feel like knots, stuck energy, tightnesses, jagged rocks, or gunkiness, and could also be termed "contractions" whereas tendencies are patterns—often obsessive and recurring—of discursive thoughts, mental pictures, or agitated emotions. In both cases, it's as if something within has been stirred up like a whirlwind.

At this point, we'd do well to be very concrete. Suppose that while you're in the midst of completing a task, one of three things happens. Either you don't want to do it because you don't like *the task*, or you don't like this particular *someone* with whom you work, or, more abstractly yet no less vividly, you don't like this specific group, organization, or *institution* that's implicated in this action.

Start the inquiry simply. Try to pick out who or what you dislike. Then consider: "Did I *actually* see the burgeoning or festering dislike, or did I miss it? If I *did* see it, then can I just take note of that dislike, of the fact that I dislike this task or this person or this organization?" Don't yet do anything with the dislike; don't push it, or pull it, or manipulate it, or mangle it. Just take note of it. Indeed, to just take note is, by virtue of standing as a quiet, open observer, to cease indulging the mind's churning.

Secondly, can you turn *inside* the body and start to feel that gunkiness in the chest, solar plexus, stomach, or elsewhere, or—alternatively—can you simply witness the whirling of thoughts or the particular qualities or edges of the feelings? This turning within, trust me, won't likely be pleasant and it may be quite intense, but it will be edifying and, in the final analysis, deeply clarifying and cleansing.

Thirdly, can you inquire now or when you have a quiet moment later on by asking yourself: "What is it about this task, this person, or this organization that really gets my goat? Why is it that every time I'm assigned this sort of task, or every time I have to work with 'someone like him,' or every time I am engaged with 'a firm like that' that my thoughts start turning, even churning?" Take time with this question; really zoom out with the aim of understanding.

Finally, after this perhaps lengthy inquiry, consider: "Can I just let experiences come and go without allowing my attention to fixate, pool, or clutch at anything?" Try it—and then notice as you return to the task *from this place of quietness* that it can now be undertaken either without any hitch or, at least, without any great stirring or rustling. See the axe chopping wood, the breath gently falling, fingers simply typing.

A retrospective: zoom out once more and try to fish out a smidgen of gratitude. Start small and be genuine. Had it not been for this particular situation appearing just as it did, how could you have begun to recognize just how often and how much you've disliked this sort of thing, that kind of person, or this type of place? How would your lifelong suffering have ever—and here so starkly—revealed itself to you? Without this piece of work, for how long might you have *remained* in the dark? The real work of work, you see, is the clearing of the mind.

You're beginning to clean up the tensions and tendencies that, ancient in origin and fiercely destructive, have been running roughshod over your life. But this is only Part 1.

❧ 8 ❧
CLEANING UP THE MIND, PART 2: THE MONSTER OF DESIRE

POINTER 9: CONSIDER: "HOW DOES IT FEEL WHEN A DESIRE APPEARS AND THE MIND GALLOPS OFF"?

POINTER 10: ASK YOURSELF: "CAN I STOP FEEDING THIS DESIRE?"

DESIRE AND DESIRELESSNESS

Although I began my discussion of the practice of inner clearing with the topic of aversions, it's commonplace for karma yoga to single out our stallion-like attachment to results, and this with good reason. A moment's reflection will show that it can seem *almost im-*

possible to act in any vigorous way without holding strongly onto the desire for a particular result. I want what shall be *mine*; I want *personal gain*.

And yet, precisely the opposite of this strenuous squeezing onto desired results is what karma yoga enjoins: we are, *The Bhagavad Gita* tells us, to act with the utmost energy without wanting or clinging to any fruits or personal gains at all. Is this even possible, or is it just pompous spiritual nonsense?

Best to tack back, as has been our approach so far, and not get ahead of ourselves. In lieu of engaging in a philosophical debate about the merits and demerits of this view of non-attachment, why not actually examine our desires and, in particular, the subset of desires that arise in the context of a mundane task to be fulfilled?

See that when you perform any mundane task, what creeps in *before* and *after* the act is— if not a strong dislike—then a *desire for good results for you or for yours*. Right now, think of any mundane task, whatever that may be, and then conjure up a desire that seems, habitually so, to precede or succeed this sort of task. What is that desire? Clarify it for yourself.

Then examine: "What does this attachment to a particular outcome really *feel like* 'from the inside'?" Put it under a microscope and observe the feeling of unrest, the searching thoughts, the sense that you have left your seat and thus have lost control, stability, equipoise. Watch very clearly the nervous ticks, the repetitive acts that ensue: the number of times you check your phone, the number of times you scan certain messages, the roaming eyes and feet and hands, the general mood of unsettledness.

How, indeed, *does* it feel when the mind gallops off and elliptically ambles back, gallops off and circles back–again and again and again? Nobody, not even the Buddha, needs to tell you that desire is the seed from which misery sprouts because you can experience this truth for yourself. To be in a state of desire is truly, and by your own reckoning, to be unfree: indeed, to be held captive *by* your captivation.

"Well," you might rebut, "then is one to simply sit around and do nothing?" This huffy reply misses the first point, which is that work is impossible to avoid and thus it'll keep finding you, no matter how hard you try to avoid it, as well as the second point about the mundanity of tasks that keep beseeching you.

"Then we're doomed," you go on melodramatically. Not at all. It's not *the act itself* that is problematic but the tendencies and tensions that *bookend the act* that drag in all the trouble. Knowing this is good news because we can learn how to "work with work." In the foreground, work unfolds however it does while in the background our study of ourself blooms, grows, takes shape, and ultimately takes over.

How, in particular, are we to approach desire? Merely by witnessing it and–the harder part–by ceasing to feed it. To witness the monster of desire–that is, how big desire is, how much we want, how insatiable it appears–is the first step. The second is, at least for a time, to exhibit self-restraint by no longer giving a free pass to obsessive thoughts, intense feelings, and habitual actions that surround any particular task.

I'm not telling you to suppress any of these thoughts or feelings, only to so keenly witness them as to know that you are beyond them. When you experience your being as being *beyond* these desires, you'll start to taste a state of desirelessness.

"And what is that state like," you might ask. It is peace, stillness, immediate and immense clarity. It is sweetness.

❧ 9 ❧
CLEANING UP THE MIND, PART 3: THE HUMILITY OF INSIGHT

POINTER 11: ASK YOURSELF: "WHAT HAVE I OVERLOOKED? HOW COME, TILL NOW, I DIDN'T SEE ALL THIS?"

CLEANSING HUMILITY

No discussion of cleaning up the mind would be complete without saying something about humility, a topic that can scarcely be overlooked once we reflect on the overall character of our aversions and our attachments, our persistent dislikes of others as well as our monstrously strong desires for something else or more or better.

As you step back, you may be struck first with a sense of disillusionment and only then with an even profounder humility. The first shock is that you thought other people were like X but they turn out, on closer inspection, to be like not-X; you thought work was like Y but the evidence reveals not-Y; you thought institutions were like Z but they're not at all like this. It may feel, disorientingly so, as if the scales are falling from your eyes. If so, this is a good thing.

The second shock impels an inward turn: the disillusionment with other things and beings gives rise, in a subtle or whipsaw-like way, to the subsequent realization concerning how impaired your judgment has been, how blind *you* have been. This dumbfoundedness ripens into humility. For a lucid example of what I have in mind, listen to Elizabeth Bennet, the protagonist in Jane Austen's novel *Pride and Prejudice*: "'Till this moment,'" she exclaims upon reading Darcy's letter because some of her prejudices have hereby been exposed, "'I never knew myself.'" Austen tellingly describes the pain Elizabeth feels just then not as resentment, frustration, or anger but as shame. As she read the letter, Elizabeth "grew absolutely ashamed of herself."

Try to feel what I'm about to say. "I had," you might think in earnest, "no idea how much downright hatred I've been holding in my heart and for so long: hatred of 'petty, bullshit tasks,' of morally unscrupulous people, of shameless self-promoters, of pretentious institutions." Now hear this same statement again, though this time with the accent mark placed on the experience of hatred—indeed, on the experience of *being* the hate-filled one. Go ahead and read it once more.

Squirming in your seat, you might experience a very strong urge to turn away from this experience of hatred. "I feel," you might observe, "that I just can't be still. I'm dragged away by the desire to flee."

And yet, you *do* turn back. As you rouse the courage required to stay with the matter at hand, you might express perplexity: "How could I have been so blind, so confused, so out of touch, so out to sea? How come I didn't see all this before? And who am I such that all of this could have been obscured?" You may very well feel as if you're waking up to your life, to the rawness of living. If so, this too is a very good thing.

But how can humility be cleansing? "Seeing," as the late Buddhist teacher Rob Burbea aptly stated, "is freeing." In this case, you begin to *separate yourself*, your being, from these predilections, judgments, knowledge claims, and errors not through willful or erroneous dissociation but through keen insight. Humility releases, severs, unburdens, opens up. To see is not to be; to see, also, is to let be. In humility, you don't shrink away; you unhook and sink back.

What I'm describing is, in a sense, like vomiting up toxins: the experience of wrenching is body-shaking, heaving, enervating, yet the quiet stillness felt on the other side of the convulsions is very precious. Humility leads to the kind of peace that's found at the bottom of a dark, murky well. It is exquisitely beautiful down here.

10

THE COMPLAINT OR THE
BLESSING OF THE
HEART

THE WISEST LOVE

The journey through work is not any kind of love story. It's not about puppy love, nor about love at first sight, nor is it the glowing love of a mother for her newborn daughter. Unlike these enthralling and, in some sense, "easy" loves, this story about work is ultimately about *wise—and therefore gritty—love*.

You see, perhaps you didn't know, when you first started reading this book, that there *was* a complaint lodged deeply in your heart. You didn't acknowledge, at first, that you were rejecting this very offering (that is, whichever task is before you just now), nor was it clear that in this rejection was a symbolic turning away from "the ways of the world." When you turn away from what's given to you, in what sense aren't you turning your back on the world? And how does it feel to turn your back, to feel as if you won't abide, oblige, or serve? Do you want to escape or to burn the whole world down?

This complaint of the heart may run deep indeed. I know it, and you will too. True, you may not want to face your lingering, latent misgivings about how your life has turned out or about what an ordinary workday—and thus your life more generally—actually *feels like*. I know that feeling too. And so, it seems, did Max Weber, who during a public talk he gave in 1917 stated, "What is hard for modern man, and especially for the younger generation, is to measure up to workaday existence."

Perhaps you believed that work would save you or that work would be how you "put your dent in the universe," and now, years or decades later, you may feel that the workaday slog, or churning, or grind is simply about managing overwhelm. This, alas, and nothing more. If you had your druthers, you'd be out of it all. That is, you'd opt out for good.

And this is not all. As you get older, you can't help but feel gently passed by too. Are you irrelevant now? Have the young barbarians come, already, to usurp you? And where has your energy, your zest gone? Your sense of the mission? Your drive?

What I'm calling "the complaint of the heart" is *the refusal to embrace wholeheartedly* the work that's been given to you. I don't mean that you don't complete it, but is it not often a *halfhearted* endeavor? How often and in which shadowy ways have you been dragging your heels because your heart hasn't been in it, not entirely?

I want you to know that your heart needn't be set in this dour direction and thus doesn't have to be closed. You have a momentous existential choice, one that comes right at the end of cleaning up the mind. As you clean up the mind, you come, in the end, to this existential choice: can I really give my entire heart to this very task, to this set of tasks, to this project, to this day, to this life?

And here is where the blessing comes. You *can*, if only you surrender. Could you, just this once, accept—without flinching and without grumbling—this very assignment? Can you, after you've crawled through the "500 yards" of mind muck, look upon this person with innocent eyes? Can you approach this very moment with lightness, openness, and softness?

In short, can you say, "Yes," in the most immediate, intuitive way possible?

In what I've written, I don't mean to imply
that you can never leave this workplace or that
career path. Know that I'm speaking here only
of *the nature, the quality of your heart*. If you can
stay with an open heart, then stay. If you can
leave with a resounding "Yes," then leave. Either way, to see *all* as a complaint or as a
blessing is what's centrally in focus.

To ask the question again: "Can you say,
'Yes,' immediately and wholeheartedly?" If you
can, then you'll understand, because you'll
know firsthand, the blessing of the heart. To
receive the blessing of the heart is to be in the
presence of love. I told you that the beginning
is not the ending: you must go *through* "the age
of experience"—the muck, the gunk, the hurts
—so that you can embrace wholeheartedly
"the second age of innocence."

I'm not asking you "to love work" in the
ordinary sense in which people toss around
this infinitive phrase. I'm inviting you to love
reality. For I want you to *know* this second innocence. It is, in truth, none other than the
wisest, and therefore deepest, love.

11

CHOP WOOD, CARRY WATER

POINTER 12: CARRY ON IN EASE.

POINTER 13: ACCEPT FULLY AND LOVE COMPLETELY.

THE LOVE OF BEING

"*Il faut imaginer Sisyphe heureux*," concludes Albert Camus's *The Myth of Sisyphus*. "One must imagine Sisyphus happy." Camus has left Sisyphus, whose fate is to keep pushing a boulder up a mountain, only to have it fall back down again, "at the foot of the mountain!" He goes on: "One always finds one's burden again."

We, however, are not Sisyphus. Our life is, like his, a fundamentally spiritual journey, yet it is not one that's defined by the same absurd movements. Rather, though ours does involve taking up hardships, the terminus is not so much a dubious attitude termed "happiness" as it is a settled condition that at first feels like ease but later on ripens into love.

For once your heart is humbled, you can return to the business of living without flinching or fancies. I'd like to speak of glimpses of ease. Haven't we all had them? And thanks to the practice of the yoga of work, couldn't these glimpses be even clearer, more vibrant, higher resolution?

"Through work," declares Swami Satprakashananda in *Mind According to Vedanta*, "you go beyond work." Following the cleaning up of the mind and, most especially, the steadying embrace of humility is grace, an understatedly beautiful experiential understanding of ease. Little by little, one finds, in particular, that one is able to carry on a certain task (and, soon enough, *any* task) *with a quiet spirit*.

"To carry on," in the sense I mean, is to feel that one is not a doer, that there's "nobody doing anything," and that there's just an "axe splitting wood," just a "bucket carrying water." "To carry on" is to make no fuss, as though a brush saturated with paint were, without any resistance or giddiness, simply gliding across a canvas.

Carry on. See, and carry on. Take note, and carry on. Let carrying on carry on. Does this make sense? Maybe a verse from *The Tao Te Ching* will help to illuminate what it's like to simply carry on *as a nameless one*:

> *Therefore the sage goes about doing*
> *nothing, teaching no talking.*
> *The ten thousand things rise and fall*
> *without cease,*
> *Creating, yet not possessing,*
> *Working, yet not taking credit,*
> *Work is done, then forgotten.*
> *Therefore it lasts forever.*
> —*"Chapter 2," The Tao Te Ching,*
> *trans. Feng and English*

"WORK IS DONE, THEN FORGOTTEN." ALL phenomena, including work, rise and fall, rise and fall without cease. Work, then, continues as is its wont, mundane tasks do not go away,

43

but there is *now* the freedom of ease in this. Isn't that so?

Without monstrous desires, without disturbing aversions, and, above all, without that demon called "pride" or "arrogance," the sage goes along while scarcely being noticed. He doesn't even think to take credit or to assign blame, doesn't know a thing about gain or loss. Just working, just creating, then leaving be. Working, creating, leaving be... Nor, don't we see?, does he ask for different work, for better work, for anything else or more or other. What is it like to ask for nothing, to need nothing, to hold onto nothing, in a sense *to be nothing*?

A story from the life of the Indian saint Anandamayi Ma (1896-1982) might add texture and color to this rough sketch of the Taoist sage. In 1909 at age 13, Anandamayi Ma was married to Ramani Mohan Cakravarti. A year later, she went to live in her parents-in-law's house, where she was tasked with fulfilling the customary household duties of a daughter-in-law. We read in Alexander Lipski's biography included in *The Essential Sri Anandamayi Ma: Life and Teachings of a 20th Century Indian Saint* that both parents-in-law

" became exceedingly fond of the little Mother of Smiles who adapted Herself to her new environment, charming everyone with Her joyfulness. She took over practically all the household chores and soon excelled in spinning, needlework, weaving, and especially in cooking. She worked so hard at scrubbing pots and keeping the house clean that her hands were covered with bruises. Many years later, when Her fame had already spread all over India, She met with Her sister-in-law, and the two exchanged happy reminiscences about village life in Sripur. Anandamayi Ma acted completely naturally, as though She was still the young village girl.

Pace Camus, we don't need to imagine Anandamayi Ma happy, since it is self-evident that she was, in all she did, experiencing the very same taste: the joy, the ease, the love of being.

. . .

"WORK IS DONE, THEN FORGOTTEN." HOW sweetly beautiful. Can *we*, starting now, hear this subtle lesson, letting it soak its softly spoken beauty down, down, down into our hearts?

If we can carry on not with strain but, more and more, with gracefulness and ease, letting work unfold before it's gently forgotten, then we'll find loving *good*. How?

To be at ease is to accept fully, and to accept fully is to love completely. For anyone who comes to regard work not as a task but, ultimately, as a movement, a brushstroke, a flourish of reality, work can no longer sever him from whatever is blessed, holy, or complete. Work, for the sage whose heart is full, is an expression of reality just as much as any other activity. To chop wood and carry water with lightness in one's heart is to love *what is*.

And this is one of the greatest truths there is: the only true love *is* the love of what is.

ACKNOWLEDGMENTS

Special thanks to Paul Millerd of The Pathless Path and to Daniel Doyon, founder of Readwise, both of whom, in their own ways, pressed me to put myself out there by writing punchy, highly relevant books. *Chop Wood, Carry Water* is the first in this series.

ABOUT THE AUTHOR

Andrew Taggart is a Ph.D.-trained practical philosopher and nondual teacher. Over the past 15 years, he's explored—with what he endearingly refers to as "high-performing weirdos"—the things that matter most (philosophy) as well as the deep peace that's at the heart of our experience (meditation). He's also a co-founder of The Inward Turn Institute. You can learn more about him by visiting inwardturninstitute.com.

www.ingramcontent.com/pod-product-compliance
Lightning Source LLC
Chambersburg PA
CBHW070647130626
46555CB00006B/2759

* 9 7 9 8 9 9 3 5 6 6 2 1 4 *